Little Sister Lozen

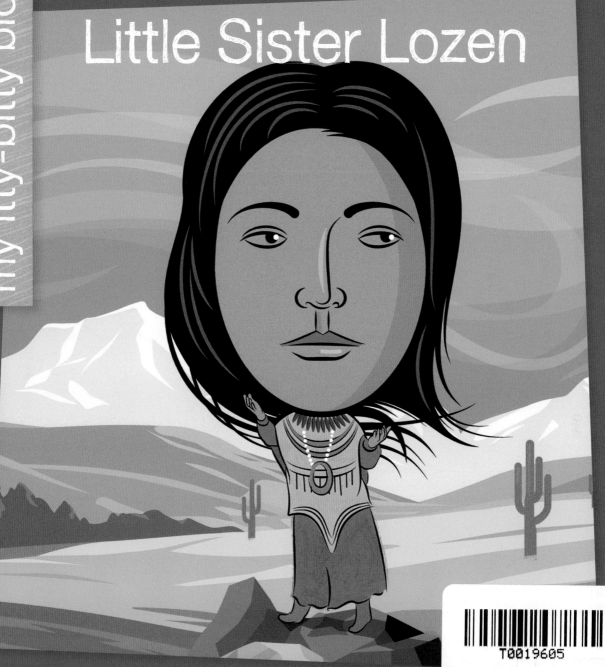

Published in the United States of America by Cherry Lake Publishing Group
Ann Arbor, Michigan
www.cherrylakepublishing.com

Reading Adviser: Beth Walker Gambro, MS, Ed., Reading Consultant, Yorkville, IL
Book Designer: Jennifer Wahi
Illustrator: Jeff Bane

Photo Credits: © a. V. ley/Shuttershock, 5; © lns1122/Flickr, 7; © Denver Public Library Digital Collections/Call No. X-32855, 9; © Denver Public Libarry Digital Collections/X-32819, 11; © National Archives Catalog/National Archives Identifier 530902, 13; © Rolling Thunder/Wikimedia, 15; © Public Domain/Wikimedia, 17, 22; © Everett Collection/Shuttershock, 19, 23; © Uploaded by prison warder?/Wikimedia, 21; Cover, 1, 6, 8, 10, Jeff Bane; Various frames throughout, © Shutterstock Images

Cherry Lake Press is an imprint of Cherry Lake Publishing Group.

Library of Congress Cataloging-in-Publication Data

Names: Thiele, June, author. | Bane, Jeff, 1957- illustrator.
Title: Little sister Lozen / by June Thiele ; illustrator, Jeff Bane.
Description: Ann Arbor, Michigan : Cherry Lake Publishing, [2023] | Series: My itty-bitty bio
Identifiers: LCCN 2022009919 | ISBN 9781668910498 (paperback) | ISBN 9781668908891 (hardcover) | ISBN 9781668913673 (pdf) | ISBN 9781668912089 (ebook)
Subjects: LCSH: Lozen, approximately 1840-1889--Juvenile literature. | Apache women--Biography--Juvenile literature. | Geronimo, 1829-1909--Friends and associates--Juvenile literature. | Apache Indians--Wars--Juvenile literature.
Classification: LCC E99.A6 T453 2023 | DDC 979.004/97250092 [B]--dc23/eng/20220506
LC record available at https://lccn.loc.gov/2022009919

Printed in the United States of America
Corporate Graphics

About the author: June Thiele writes and acts in Chicago where they live with their wife and child. June is Dena'ina Athabascan and Yup'ik, Indigenous cultures of Alaska. They try to get back home to Alaska as much as possible.

About the illustrator: Jeff Bane and his two business partners own a studio along the American River in Folsom, California, home of the 1849 Gold Rush. When Jeff's not sketching or illustrating for clients, he's either swimming or kayaking in the river to relax.

I was born around 1840. My people are **Native American**. I was part of the **Apache tribe**.

I looked up to my brother, Victorio.
He was an important **chief**.
I wanted to be like him. I wanted
to be a leader and a warrior. His
nickname for me was "Little Sister."

What are your dreams?

I was not like most women. I did not want to marry. I did not want to stay home. I wanted to fight and protect others. I was good at finding our enemies.

I also knew about medicine.
I was a **shaman**. I was a healer.

What do you like learning about?

I protected my people from **colonizers**. They were trying to take our land. My brother and I fought back.

We were pushed off our land. We were forced to live in a harsh area.

I helped many people. I helped scared women and children. They were inspired by me. They saw my strength.

I fought alongside Geronimo after my brother was killed. Geronimo was a great warrior. But we eventually **surrendered**.

19

I died at age 50 in prison from sickness. I fought hard for my people. My **legacy** lives on in my culture.

What would you like to ask me?

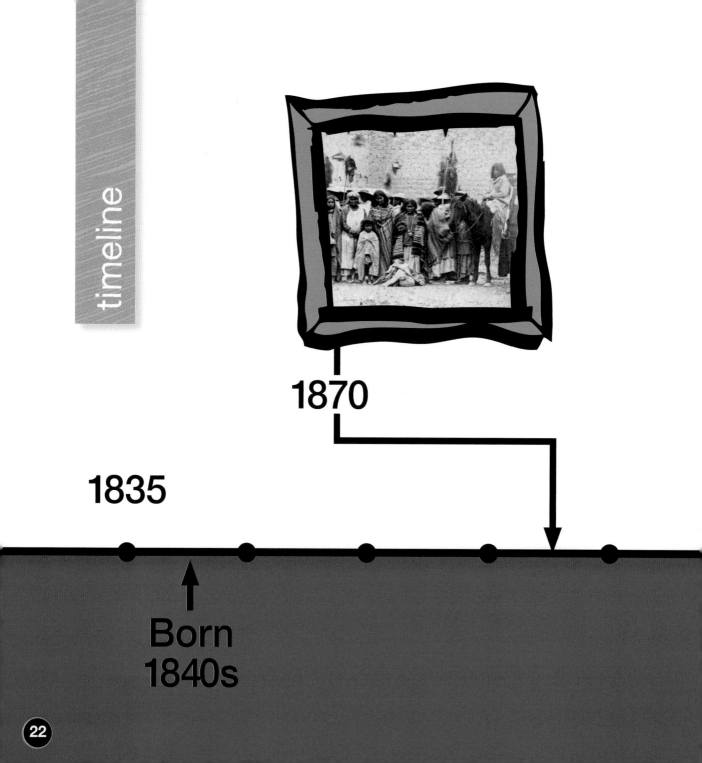

1870

1835

Born
1840s

1886

1935

Died
1889

glossary

Apache (uh-PAH-chee) Native American people who lived in the southwestern part of the United States

chief (CHEEF) a leader of a tribal community or a clan

colonizers (KAH-luh-nye-zuhrz) nations or states that take control of a people or area

legacy (LEH-guh-see) something handed down from one generation to another

Native American (NAY-tiv uh-MER-uh-kuhn) one of the people who originally lived in America, or a relative of these people

shaman (SHAH-muhn) a healer who also serves as a spiritual adviser

surrendered (suh-REN-durd) gave up

tribe (TRYB) a group of people including many families, clans, or generations

index